DISCARDED

Aboriginal Legends of Canada

Métis

Megan Cuthbert

Weigl

Published by Weigl Educational Publishers Limited
6325 10th Street SE
Calgary, Alberta T2H 2Z9

Website: www.weigl.ca

Library and Archives Canada Cataloguing in Publication available upon request.
Fax 403-233-7769 for the attention of the Publishing Records department.

ISBN 978-1-77071-566-0 (hardcover)
ISBN 978-1-77071-567-7 (softcover)
ISBN 978-1-77071-568-4 (multi-user ebook)

Printed in the United States of America in North Mankato, Minnesota
1 2 3 4 5 6 7 8 9 0 17 16 15 14 13

072013
WEP130613

Project Coordinator: Heather Kissock
Editor: Alexis Roumanis
Designer: Mandy Christiansen
Illustrator: Martha Jablonski-Jones

Photo Credits
Weigl acknowledges Alamy and Getty Images as its primary image suppliers for this title.

We gratefully acknowledge the financial support of the Government of Canada through the Canada Book Fund for our publishing activities.

CONTENTS

Meet the Métis

Métis is a French word that means "mixed." The name Métis was given to the children of European and **First Nations** parents. The Métis played important roles as guides and **fur traders**, and many of their traditions are based on these roles. Today, more than 400,000 Métis live throughout the country.

Storytelling has always been an important part of Métis life. Grandmothers or grandfathers would gather children by the fireplace or around a campfire at night to tell stories. The stories were a bridge between the children's First Nations **heritage** and their Métis community. Storytellers would sometimes compete with each other to see who could tell the most interesting tale.

Stories of Creation

The Métis have many stories that explain how the universe and its parts were created. Some of these stories feature a character called Wisahkecahk. Storytellers taught lessons through the adventures of Wisahkecahk. Wisahkecahk is a creature that is able to talk to any living thing, and is often very wise.

Métis stories often have a combination of popular characters from different First Nations groups.

How the Moon Came to Be is a Métis story about the creation of the Moon. The story tells what happens when Wisahkecahk sees that the Sun has not appeared in the sky. His solution to the problem brings a new form of light to the sky.

Wisahkecahk is said to have travelled to the Moon by hanging on to the legs of a crane.

Objects in the sky, such as the Moon and stars, hold spiritual significance to Canada's Aboriginal Peoples.

How the MOON Came to Be

In the beginning, the only light in the sky was the Sun. There was no Moon. The Caretaker of the Sun made sure the Sun shone brightly by burning a great fire all day long.

The Caretaker was getting old. One day, he sat down with his two children and made them promise to keep the fire burning. He explained that if the fire did not burn, all the people and animals on Earth would die. Shortly after talking with his children, the Caretaker died.

Now it was the children's job to start the Sun's fire. When morning came the next day, the children began arguing over who should start the Sun's fire. The people on Earth started to worry when the Sun did not appear that day. They sent Wisahkecahk to the Sun to see what was happening. When Wisahkecahk arrived on the Sun, he separated the fighting children and gave each of them the job of keeping a fire burning. The boy was to keep the Sun's fire burning all day, and the girl would keep a different fire burning at night. That is how the Moon came to be.

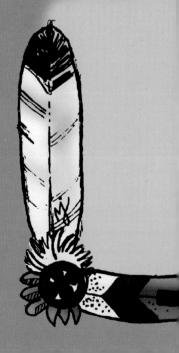

Nature Stories

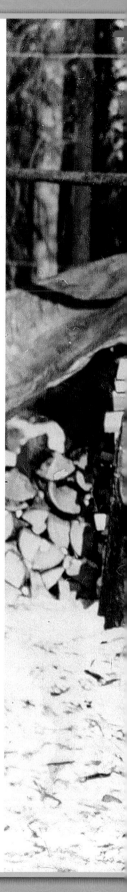

Stories are often used as a way of explaining the **natural world**. Sometimes, these stories, or **legends,** explain why an animal looks or acts a certain way. Other stories explain the geography of an area. These stories were helpful for Métis who travelled across the country as guides and traders.

The Legend of the Tamarack tells of how the tamarack tree became a source of medicine for the Métis. The Métis used the tree to heal many medical conditions. Like many **Aboriginal** groups, the Métis believed that every living thing has a spirit. The story of the tamarack explains that the creatures of Earth are meant to help each other.

The Métis used the bark of the tamarack to treat cuts, sores, and frostbite.

Métis trappers often ventured deep into the woods to set their traps. They relied on the plants and animals around them for survival.

The LEGEND of the TAMARACK

A flock of birds were flying south for the winter when a storm began. The birds looked for shelter and saw the tamarack trees. The tamaracks were very beautiful. They had thick branches and soft needles to keep them warm. The tamaracks were also very proud of their looks. They did not want the birds sitting on them. When the birds came to them, the tamaracks closed their branches and would not let them land.

The Great Spirit decided to teach the tamaracks a lesson. As they refused to help shelter their fellow creatures, the Great Spirit decided that the tamaracks would not have shelter from the cold either. He made their needles fall off in the cold months of winter.

The tamaracks regretted what they had done. To make up for their selfishness, they decided to help the people who lived on their land. The Great Spirit gave the tamaracks the ability to heal. Aboriginal People have used the trees as an important source of medicine ever since.

Life Lessons

Some Métis stories were used to teach a lesson or explain how people should behave. The Métis would often tell stories at family and community gatherings. Older Métis would use stories to explain to younger Métis how they should act and what would happen if they did not behave properly.

The Métis often tell their stories through music. They have a specific type of music, which is based around the Métis fiddle. The Métis style of fiddling is very quick and upbeat, and the words often contain a Métis legend.

How the People Hunted the Moose shows why people should respect the moose. Like all of Canada's Aboriginal People, the Métis have great respect for the animal world. In the past, they relied on animals for clothing, food, and tools. The Métis were always careful to only hunt as many animals as they needed and to use all parts of the animal. They honoured the animals because they helped the Métis survive.

Métis women would stretch and dry moosehides so they could be turned into coats, leggings, and hats.

Moose are found throughout Canada. They live in the country's forests, mountains, and tundra regions.

How the PEOPLE Hunted the MOOSE

A family of moose were sitting in their lodge when a pipe came floating through the door. The old moose knew that humans used this pipe to ask for success in their hunt. The old moose warned the young moose that the humans would now know where to find them. The young moose was not worried. He believed he could outrun the people.

The next day, the hunters found the young moose. He tried to outrun the hunters, but was slowed by the heavy snow.

The hunters caught the young moose. They thanked him for giving himself to them so they could survive. They soothed his spirit and treated his body carefully.

The spirit of the young moose told the other moose that the hunters had treated him with respect. To to this day, hunters that show respect for the moose are the ones who are successful in their hunt.

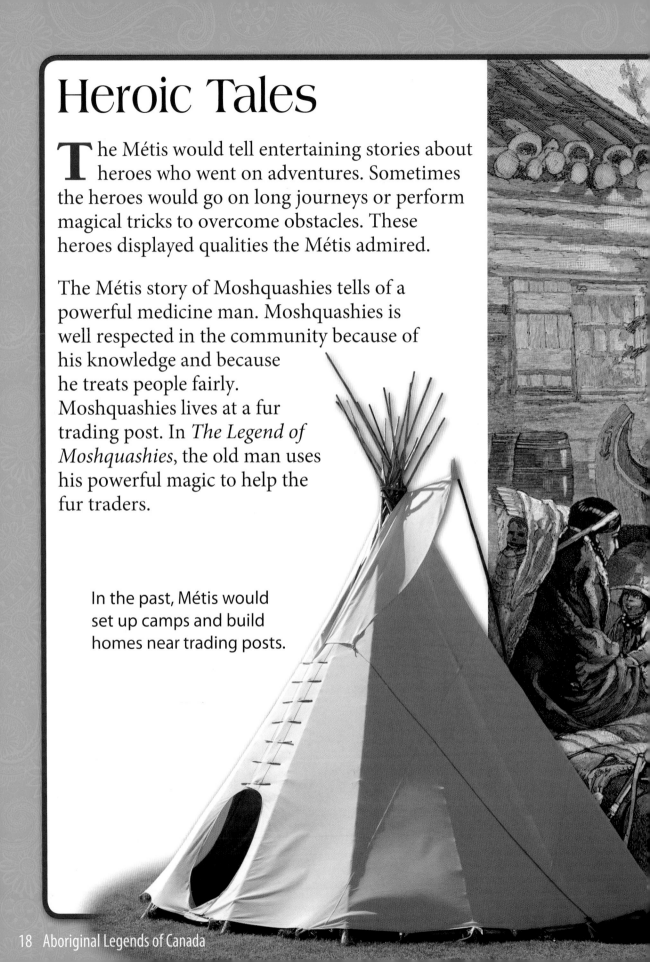

Heroic Tales

The Métis would tell entertaining stories about heroes who went on adventures. Sometimes the heroes would go on long journeys or perform magical tricks to overcome obstacles. These heroes displayed qualities the Métis admired.

The Métis story of Moshquashies tells of a powerful medicine man. Moshquashies is well respected in the community because of his knowledge and because he treats people fairly. Moshquashies lives at a fur trading post. In *The Legend of Moshquashies*, the old man uses his powerful magic to help the fur traders.

In the past, Métis would set up camps and build homes near trading posts.

Trading posts were stocked with various goods to trade with Aboriginal People who brought furs.

The Legend of MOSHQUASHIES

Moshquashies was an old man who held great power. Every time Moshquashies died, he came back more powerful than before. One day, traders came to the post where Moshquashies lived. They complained about a woman who was making people pay money to pass her house on their way from Hudson Bay. If the people did not pay her, she would bring them bad luck.

Moshquashies became angry when he heard the story. He asked the men to take him to the woman in their canoe. When they arrived, the woman demanded payment from him. Moshquashies told her that she could not charge people for passing by. He then returned to the canoe and left.

The woman sent a large cloud of insects to attack the canoe. Moshquashies took a deep breath and blew through his medicine bag toward the insects. The insects flew away. Next, the woman sent a storm over the lake. Moshquashies blew through his medicine bag, and the clouds disappeared. The men made it back home safely.

Activity

Make your own Métis-style sash bracelet.

The Métis were known for wearing colourful sashes around their waists. These sashes became an important symbol of Métis **culture**.

You Will Need:

needle

thread

coloured wool skeins

1. Cut three pieces of the same coloured wool and braid them together.

2. Make more braids from the other colours of wool.

3. When you have completed the braids, sew the different coloured braids together lengthwise to make a multi-coloured sash bracelet.

Further Research

Many books and websites provide information on the Métis and their legends. To learn more about this topic, borrow books from the library, or search the internet.

Books

Most libraries have computers that connect to a database for researching information. If you input a key word, you will be provided with a list of books in the library that contain information on that topic. Non-fiction books are arranged numerically, using their call number. Fiction books are organized alphabetically by the author's last name.

Websites

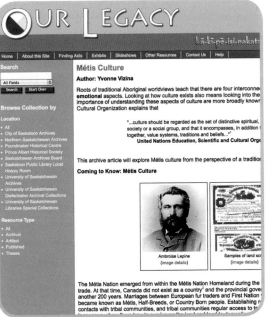

Learn more about Métis history at: http://www.collectionscanada. gc.ca/settlement/kids/021013-2081-e.html

To read more about the Métis culture, visit: www.scaa.sk.ca/ourlegacy/exhibit_metisculture

Key Words

Aboriginal: First Nations, Inuit, and Métis of Canada

culture: the arts, beliefs, and habits of a community, people, or country

First Nations: members of Canada's Aboriginal community who are not Inuit or Métis

fur traders: people who traded furs for other items

heritage: the people, places, and culture of the past

legends: stories that have been passed down from generation to generation

natural world: relating to things that have not been made by people

Index